JESUS LOVES ME
BY
PRINCE ALBERT KING.
AN ILLUSTRATED CHRISTIAN NOVEL OF NONFICTION FOR KIDS FROM AGES 2 – 13 YEARS OLD

IN THE BEGINNING GOD CREATED THE HEAVENS AND THE EARTH.

GOD MADE A GARDEN CALLED EDEN.

THEN GOD MADE A MAN FROM THE DUST OF THE EARTH. THIS FIRST MAN HE CALLED

ADAM.

GENESIS 1–2 TELLS US THAT LIVING THINGS, HUMAN BEINGS INCLUDED, WERE MADE OF *DUST OF THE GROUND.* " AND

THE LORD GOD FORMED MAN OF THE DUST OF THE GROUND, AND BREATHED INTO HIS NOSTRILS THE BREATH OF LIFE; AND MAN BECAME A LIVING SOUL" (GENESIS 2:7). AND OUT OF THE GROUND, GOD FORMED EVERY BEAST OF

THE FIELD AND EVERY BIRD OF THE SKY, AND BROUGHT THEM TO THE MAN (*GENESIS 2:19*). AFTER THE FALL OF MAN THROUGH SIN (*GENESIS 3:17*), THE LORD GOD SENT MAN OUT OF THE GARDEN OF EDEN TO TILL THE

GROUND FROM WHICH HE WAS TAKEN (GENESIS *3:23*).

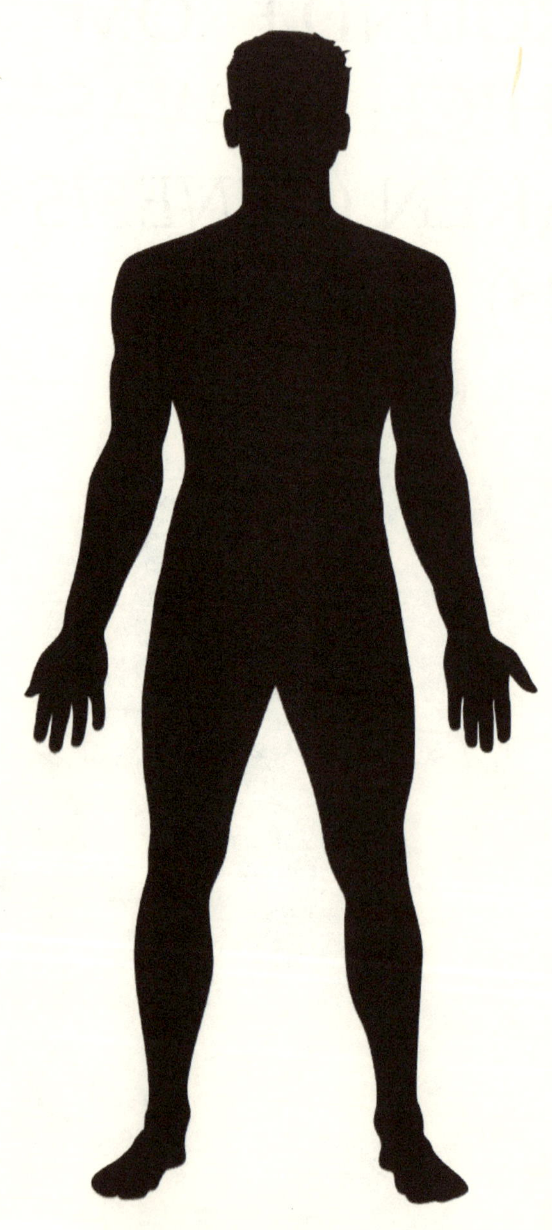

ADAM

GOD BREATHE INTO
THE NOSTRILLS OF
THE MAN THE
BREATHE OF LIFE
AND MAN BECAME
A LIVING SOUL.

THEN GOD SAID IT
IS NOT GOOD FOR
THE MAN TO BE
ALONE.
I WILL MAKE A

HELP MATE FOR HIM.

SO GOD CREATED A WOMAN.

EVE

MOTHER OF ALL
LIVING

ADAM CALLED HER NAME EVE BECAUSE SHE WAS THE MOTHER OF ALL LIVING THINGS.

GOD TOLD ADAM
NOT TO EAT FROM
A TREE HE HAD
PLACED IN THE
CENTER OF THE
GARDEN.

A SNAKE CAME TO EVE ONE DAY AND CAUSE HER TO QUESTION GOD'S WORD.

EVE ATE OF THE FRUIT AND GAVE

SOME TO ADAM. HE ATE ALSO.

THEY WERE TOLD TO LEAVE THE GARDEN AND TO NEVER RETURN. THEY LEFT BEING VERY SAD. GOD PLACED ANGELS WITH SWORDS AT THE ENTRANCE OF THE GARDEN SO THAT ADAM AND EVE COULD NOT RETURN.

THE FORBIDDEN FRUIT

ADAM AND EVE DISOBEYED GOD.

THEY WERE TOLD
TO LEAVE THE
GARDEN.

GOD PUT AN ANGEL
AT THE GATEWAY
SO THAT THEY
COULD NOT
RETURN TO EDEN.

EVEN THOUGH
MAN HAD SINNED
BY DISOBEYING

GOD'S WORD. HE STILL LOVED THEM. HE DECIDED TO HELP THEM. HE WOULD SEND HIS SON JESUS FIRST AS A BABY.

THE BABY WOULD GROW UP TO BE A MAN AND LATER DIE ON A CROSS. WHEN HE DIES GOD WOULD FORGIVE MANKIND

FOR THEIR SINS.

BOOK OF JOHN
CHAPTER 3
JOHN 3:<u>16</u> FOR GOD
SO LOVED THE
WORLD, THAT HE
GAVE HIS ONLY
BEGOTTEN SON,
THAT WHOSOEVER
BELIEVETH IN HIM
SHOULD NOT
PERISH, BUT HAVE
EVERLASTING LIFE.

<u>17</u> FOR GOD SENT NOT HIS SON INTO THE WORLD TO CONDEMN THE WORLD; BUT THAT THE WORLD THROUGH HIM MIGHT BE SAVED.

JOHN 3:1 **1** SEE WHAT GREAT LOVE THE FATHER HAS LAVISHED ON US, THAT WE SHOULD BE CALLED

CHILDREN OF GOD! AND THAT IS WHAT WE ARE! THE REASON THE WORLD DOES NOT KNOW US IS THAT IT DID NOT KNOW HIM.

1 JOHN 2:291 JOHN

31 JOHN 3:2

JER 31:3 THE LORD HATH APPEARED OF

OLD UNTO ME, SAYING, YEA, I HAVE LOVED THEE WITH AN EVERLASTING LOVE: THEREFORE WITH LOVING-KINDNESS' HAVE I DRAWN THEE.

God
is
Love

JESUS DIED.HIS
BLOOD WASHES
AWAY OUR SINS.
BUT THERE IS GOOD

NEWS. JESUS CHRIST AROSE FROM THE DEAD ON THE THIRD DAY.

Mark 10:13-16 New Living Translation (NLT)

Jesus Blesses the Children

13 One day some parents brought their children to Jesus so he could touch and bless them. But the disciples scolded the parents for bothering him.

¹⁴ When Jesus saw what was happening, he was angry with his disciples. He said to them, "Let the children come to me. Don't stop them! For the Kingdom of God belongs to those who are like these children. ¹⁵ I tell you the truth, anyone who doesn't receive the Kingdom of God like a child will never enter it." ¹⁶ Then he

took the children in his arms and placed his hands on their heads and blessed them.

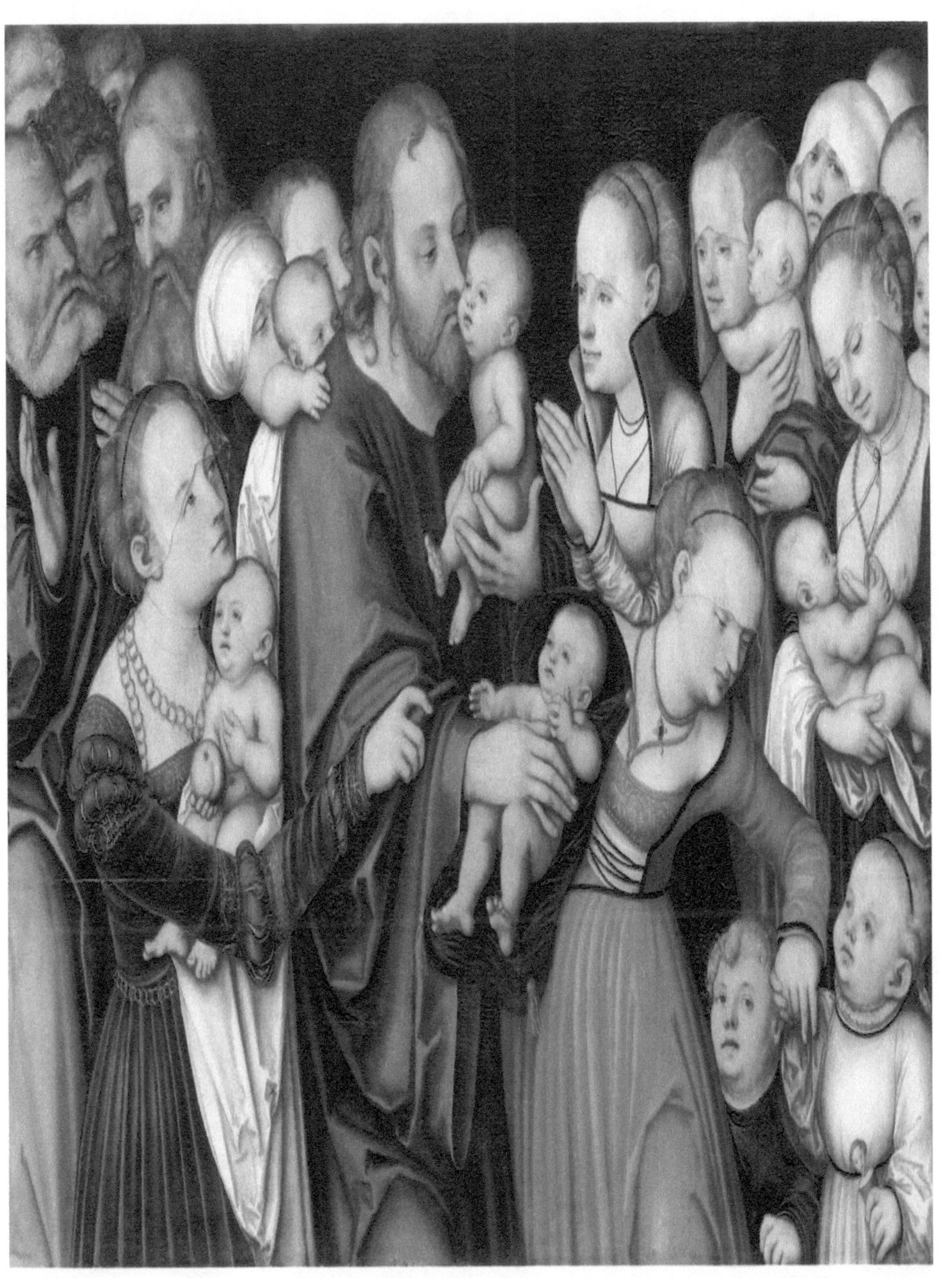

NO MATTER WHO YOU ARE,OR WHERE YOU ARE FROM GOD LOVES YOU AND GOD LOVES ME.

WHEN MOTHERS OF SALEM HYMN LYRICS

WHEN MOTHERS OF SALEM THEIR CHILDREN BROUGHT TO JESUS, THE STERN DISCIPLES DROVE THEM BACK AND BADE THEM TO DEPART:
BUT JESUS SAW THEM ERE THEY

FLED AND SWEETLY
SMILED AND
KINDLY SAID,
"SUFFER LITTLE
CHILDREN TO COME
UNTO ME."

"FOR I WILL
RECEIVE THEM AND
FOLD THEM TO MY
BOSOM:
I'LL BE A SHEPHERD
TO THESE LAMBS, O

DRIVE THEM NOT
AWAY;
FOR IF THEIR
HEARTS TO ME
THEY GIVE, THEY
SHALL WITH ME IN
GLORY LIVE:
SUFFER LITTLE
CHILDREN TO COME
UNTO ME."

HOW KIND WAS
OUR SAVIOR TO BID

THESE CHILDREN
WELCOME!
BUT THERE ARE
MANY THOUSANDS
WHO HAVE NEVER
HEARD HIS NAME;
THE BIBLE THEY
HAVE NEVER READ,
THEY KNOW NOT
THAT THE SAVIOR
SAID,
"SUFFER LITTLE
CHILDREN TO COME

UNTO ME."
O SOON MAY THE
HEATHEN OF EVERY
TRIBE AND NATION
FULFILL THY
BLESSÈD WORD AND
CAST THEIR IDOLS
ALL AWAY!
O SHINE UPON
THEM FROM ABOVE
AND SHOW
THYSELF A GOD OF
LOVE, TEACH THE

LITTLE CHILDREN TO COME UNTO THEE!

SONGS:

Yes Jesus loves me

Yes Jesus loves me for the
Bible tells me so.
Jesus loves me this I know
For the Bible tells me so
Little ones to him belong
They are weak but he is
strong

Yes Jesus loves me
Oh, yes Jesus loves me

Yes Jesus loves me for the
Bible tells me so

Pressing on the up away
Always guide me Lord I
pray, Undeserving, and
stubbornly, never fail to
love me still.

Yes Jesus loves me
Oh yes Jesus loves me
Oh yes Jesus loves me, for
the Bible tells me so
Yes Jesus loves me, love
Oh yes…
Yes Jesus loves me
Oh, yes Jesus loves me
Yes Jesus loves me for the
Bible tells me so.

JESUS ON THE CROSS

JESUS ON TRIAL

THE SINNERS PRAYER.

Dear God, I know that I am a sinner and there is nothing that I can do to save myself. I confess my complete helplessness to forgive my own sin or to work my way to **heaven**. *At this moment I trust Christ alone as the One who bore my sin when He died on the* cross. I believe that He did all that will ever be necessary for me to stand in your holy presence. I thank you that Christ was raised from the dead as a guarantee of my own resurrection. As best as I can, I now transfer my trust to Him. I am grateful that He has promised to receive me despite my many sins and failures. Father, I take *you at your word. I thank you that I can face death now that you are my Savior. Thank you for the assurance that you will walk with me through the deep valley. Thank you for hearing this prayer. In Jesus' Name. Amen.*

Prayer

IF YOU HAVE PRAYED THE SINNERS PRAYER AND TRUSTED JESUS AS YOUR LORD AND SAVIOUR, THEN:

PRAY EVERY DAY:

YOU CAN TALK TO JESUS AT ANY TIME.TELL HIM HOW YOU ARE FEELING. HE IS ALWAYS WAITING TO LISTEN TO YOU WHEN YOU PRAY.

ASK HIM FOR WHAT YOU NEED.

READ THE BIBLE EVERY DAY.START WITH THE BOOK OF JOHN. TELL YOUR FRIENDS THAT YOU HAVE ACCEPTED JESUS CHRIST INTO HEART AND YOUR LIFE.

Dr. Prince Albert King is a Bahamian Author who lives in Nassau, New Providence, Bahamas. A Preacher and third generation Police Officer. He is a widower and the father of one daughter Octavia. Prince's roots are well grounded in the beautiful tranquil Cat Island. He is a descendant of the Farrington, Stubbs and King Families of Arthur's Town (Zion Hill) and Dumfries Districts.